BACKPACKER

Outdoor
Hazards

BACKPACKER®

Outdoor
Hazards

AVOIDING TROUBLE IN
THE BACKCOUNTRY

Dave Anderson

FALCONGUIDES

GUILFORD, CONNECTICUT
HELENA, MONTANA

AN IMPRINT OF GLOBE PEQUOT PRESS

FALCONGUIDES®

Copyright © 2012 by Morris Book Publishing, LLC

Backpacker is a registered trademark of Cruz Bay Publishing, Inc.
FalconGuides is an imprint of Globe Pequot Press.
Falcon, FalconGuides, and Outfit Your Mind are registered trademarks of Morris
Book Publishing, LLC.

Photos: Dave Anderson
Text design: Sheryl P. Kober
Page layout: Justin Marciano
Project editor: Julie Marsh

Library of Congress Cataloging-in-Publication Data is available on file.

ISBN 978-0-7627-7296-4

Printed in China

10 9 8 7 6 5 4 3 2 1

Contents

Introduction

Waiting for the next strike, the three of us crouched on a steep incline just below the wide open tablelands of the Alpine Gardens on Mount Washington in the White Mountains of New Hampshire. Rain and hail lashed against my face and the wind cut through my T-shirt causing me to shake with cold. The lightning storm had us pinned down with no shelter. We had an overwhelming urge to run across the exposed terrain above us to the descent trail. Instead we stayed in the gully below, spread ourselves a few dozen feet apart, squatted on our day packs and waited. It was the best decision we had made all day. Another flash of light lit up the darkened mountainside, followed in a few seconds by a loud boom of thunder. The storm was moving away from us and the threat of being struck by lightning was diminishing.

We had survived the lightning storm, which many people would consider the main outdoor hazard of our situation that day. In reality, hypothermia, caused by the cold, wet conditions was probably a greater threat to our lives. However, being caught in the storm and becoming hypothermic were both caused by a series of small mistakes that, when added up, could have proved disastrous.

None of us had visited the White Mountains before and we were unprepared for the day hike. To start with, we had failed to check the weather forecast, which called for afternoon thunderstorms. While we knew the length of the hike in miles, we had not taken into consideration how rugged the terrain would be and how the dramatic change in elevation would slow our progress. As a result, we started our adventure much later than we should have. Our intended route was on trail, so we did not feel the need to bring a map. Later, when the main trail diverged into several unmarked trails, we spent considerable time arguing over the correct path to take. When we left the car at the trailhead, the August temperatures and the morning sun had us sweating in T-shirts and shorts, and we decided against bringing extra warm layers and rain gear. The steep terrain took us longer than we had anticipated and we quickly consumed all of our water and food. All of these factors left us cold, wet, hungry, dehydrated, and scared while crouching on the ground during an electrical storm.

Luckily for us, the summer storm passed quickly and after a few jumping jacks to warm us up, we continued across the Alpine Gardens down the Lions Head trail back to the car.

HOW TO USE THIS BOOK

While experiential education is one way of understanding the dangers in the outdoors, a safer avenue to learn about hazards is to educate yourself before you go into the backcountry. In this book we will look

Educate yourself about potential hazards before you go into the backcountry.

at both subjective and objective hazards in the outdoors. Subjective hazards are dangers that are controllable by people. Objective hazards are risks that exist in the wilderness that can be prepared for but cannot be controlled.

People's attention is often drawn to sensationalized objective outdoor hazards such as lightning, blizzards, bears, or avalanches, all of which can be extremely dangerous to the backcountry traveler. However, subjective risks like rolling an ankle on a rough trail or developing blisters from a poorly fitted pair of hiking boots are, in reality, much greater hazards to an average hiker.

The goal of this book is to identify some of the common hazards hikers and backpackers might encounter and provide ways of eliminating or reducing these hazards to have a safer and more enjoyable outdoor experience.

Chapter One
Subjective Hazards

While objective hazards—such as lightning, blizzards, and swiftly moving rivers—can exist independently of anything you might do, subjective hazards can be controlled, at least in part, by the decisions you make as a backcountry traveler.

HAZARD: LACK OF PREPARATION

For any type of outdoor activity there should be a planning session about what to bring and what skills you need before you head out in the wilds. Lack of such preparation is one of the primary hazards backcountry hikers and backpackers face.

Staying hydrated boosts energy, attitude, and acclimatization.

Water and Food

Humans have a few basic needs: water, food, and shelter. Inexperienced backcountry travelers often underestimate the amount of water needed to maintain healthy body functions. The common recommendation of consuming at least eight glasses of water per day might be appropriate if you are working in an environmentally controlled office, but woefully inadequate if you are hiking through Death Valley in July. During periods of intense exertion in hot conditions, your body can process 1 to 1.5 liters of water per hour. Signs such as thirst, decreased and darkened urine, a headache, and general fatigue are indicators that you are not ingesting enough liquids. However, you also need to ingest food to maintain adequate electrolyte balance within the cells of your body and proper glucose (sugar) levels in your blood. Carbohydrate-rich, fluid replacement drinks and gels are quickly absorbed by the body and contain important electrolytes such as calcium, potassium, and sodium. Carrying a backpack up a steep trail will burn a lot of calories. Consuming 135–270 calories of carbohydrates per hour will help maintain an adequate level of glucose in the blood. Complex carbohydrates (sugars) found in energy bars and dried fruit will provide continuous energy without the sugar crash caused by candy bars. Adding fats and protein-rich foods that digest slowly (like cheese) to evening meals will help you sleep warm throughout the night and revitalize your muscles.

Shelter, Clothing, and Footwear

Prior research into the type of terrain you will encounter, possible weather conditions, and estimated length of your adventure will determine what type of clothing, equipment, and shelter you bring. Before venturing into the backcountry on an extended trip, it is always a good idea to test out your gear beforehand to make sure things like the tent zippers are working and hiking boots are broken in. Clothing systems should include items that can be comfortably layered on top of each other, allowing hikers to easily adapt to changing weather conditions. Shelter systems (tents) should be strong enough to withstand the worst possible conditions you might face. The challenge in deciding what to bring boils down to the need to have enough gear to be safe and relatively comfortable. However, bringing too much increases

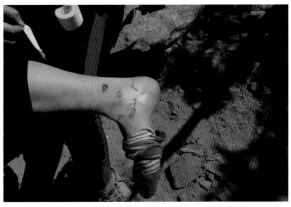

Improperly fitted boots can produce painful blisters.

your pack weight, which could lead to athletic injuries, blisters, and a general unhappy experience.

» Know the expected temperatures and likelihood of precipitation for the location during the time period of your trip.
» Determine how long your route will take to complete and bring enough water (or water treatment supplies) and food to sustain yourself.
» Bring multifunctional clothing and equipment that can be used together to increase functionality and decrease the weight of your pack.

HAZARD: GETTING IN OVER YOUR HEAD

One of the most common hazards people encounter in the backcountry is exceeding their own technical skills or abilities. Most people would agree that learning to drive a car in Manhattan in the middle of rush hour would be a bad idea. Likewise, learning how to place climbing protection when you're halfway up El Capitan in Yosemite seems equally foolish. The difference between the two examples is you can always park the car and take a taxi in New York; on El Capitan your life depends on your skill. Whether you are hiking through a boulder field, crossing a river, or kicking steps up a steep snow slope, all of these activities require competent movement skills and the knowledge of the risks associated with each type of terrain.

Outdoor travelers generally fall into one of five categories: novice, beginner, proficient, expert, and master. Novices are often unaware of what they don't know, while beginners at least realize what skills they are lacking. Proficiency is the next tier of outdoor skills, where the person has the skills and awareness but needs always to be making a conscious effort to focus on safety. The expert's skills are so well developed that they come automatically without much conscious thought. Finally, the master maintains his automatic competence by reflecting back on his skills to make improvements. Knowing which category you fall into is a primary component of not getting in over your head on a backcountry trip. The best way to avoid this hazard is to research what challenges you will face during your adventure, bring the appropriate equipment, know how to use it, and make sure your backcountry skills are sufficient for the journey.

Learn How to Use Equipment Properly

There is a plethora of outdoor gear available that can make your backcountry experiences safer and more enjoyable. You need to avoid taking too much equipment, and you need to know how to use the equipment you do bring. Some people see an ice axe as a glorified walking stick for traveling on snow and ice. In well-trained hands, however, an ice axe can be used to chop steps, ascend vertical ice, and quickly self-arrest falls on steep

snow. In the hands of a novice it is often dropped, or worse, it accidentally impales its owner during a poorly attempted self-arrest maneuver. No matter how much money you spend on the latest state-of-the art piece of gear, it does not buy automatic competence. It's up to you to seek proper instruction.

Learn Proper Navigation Skills

Each year, search and rescue organizations across the country are called to look for lost hikers. The main reason people get lost is that they fail to bring or do not know how to use navigation tools such as a map or GPS (global positioning system). While new technology, such as GPS, is a great tool to aid your navigation, being able to interpret topographical features on a map is a basic skill all wilderness users should have. Trails get rerouted, new buildings appear, others burn down, a new dam might change a river flow, but the contours of the land do not change. Looking at the three-dimensional terrain of a landscape in front of

Basic navigation skills are a must in the backcountry.

you and then trying to extrapolate that information to a two-dimensional map takes practice. However, once you hone your map-reading skills, they can be used anywhere in the world, and unlike a GPS, map-reading skills won't break or run out of batteries.

Tips to Avoid Getting In Over Your Head

» Figure out what skills are going to be needed to safely complete your intended route and make sure everyone is capable of performing these skills.
» Buy or borrow outdoor gear needed for your trip and spend time familiarizing yourself with how it operates and its limitations.
» Learn how to read a map and interpret topographic features.

HAZARD: POOR PHYSICAL CONDITIONING

Backcountry adventures can require a repertoire of technical outdoor skills. However, the core skill that many novice hikers often underestimate is how physically challenging carrying a backpack can be, especially a pack loaded with gear for several nights in the backcountry. Throw in a surprise snowstorm while crossing a large boulder field and even a seasoned backpacking veteran will have her hands full. A loss in balance, as the result of poor general fitness, can quickly turn into a sprained ankle or worse in rugged trail conditions.

Get in Shape

While running and lifting weights will increase your aerobic capacity and muscle strength, there is no better training for carrying a heavy pack other than carrying a heavy pack. Some people try to simulate the rigors

Running is a good way to get yourself in better shape for your next outdoor adventure.

of backpacking by filling a pack with some weight and regularly climbing up sets of stairs or walking around the block several times a week. Although such routines will help with getting you used to carrying a pack, the main thing they lack is duration. A typical backpacking day usually consists of carrying a pack for at least six to eight hours and the wear and tear on muscles and joints is cumulative over time. Before venturing out on a two-week section of the Appalachian Trail, a long weekend excursion with a fully loaded pack is a great shakedown trip. You can see what muscles and joints are the most impacted and then train specifically to strengthen that area of your body.

The best way to train for a backpacking trip is to go on a short backpacking trip!

HAZARD: PRE-EXISTING MEDICAL CONDITIONS

Pre-existing medical conditions should be carefully evaluated before attempting any outdoor adventure. Obviously, people with heart conditions, diabetes, or other serious health concerns should seek advice from their physicians. Also, people's backs, knees, ankles, and other joints can be weakened by age, previous injuries, or genetics, and these impairments need to be taken into account during the planning stages of a backcountry trip. Fortunately, there are several resources available to ease the wear and tear on the body. Today there is a tremendous amount of high-quality, extremely lightweight gear available for consumers that can drastically reduce pack weight. Trekking poles are great for incorporating the arms when ascending steep trail, helping cushion the knees and ankles during steep descents, and maintaining balance in rough terrain. For longer excursions into the wilds, horses, llamas, goats, and even human porters can be hired to carry camping gear, leaving you with just a daypack on your back.

HAZARD: PHOBIAS AND FEARS

For every kind of outdoor activity or environment, there is a named phobia associated with it, from hydrophobia, the fear of water, to xerophobia, the fear of dry places. Fear of potentially dangerous activities or

When planning an adventure make sure you are comfortable with the terrain you will encounter.

environmental conditions is a normal, healthy, human reaction. However, the definition of a phobia is an irrational fear that affects a person's daily actions. Knowing what aspects of the outdoor environment make you uncomfortable will help you choose appropriate objectives and is key to having a pleasant experience. You do not want to hike up the exposed Angels Landing trail in Zion National Park only to discover you have acrophobia (fear of heights) and be frozen in place with fear halfway up the trail.

While some people enjoy traveling in the backcountry to escape the stresses of the modern world, outdoor adventures often have their own challenges. Trying to wrap up personal issues and work deadlines before you head into the wilderness will allow you to be more present on your outdoor trip. Having a clear mind will allow you to enjoy the environment around you and the people in your group, and to focus on safely traveling in the backcountry.

HAZARD: PROBLEMS IN COMMUNICATION AND DECISION MAKING

During a weekend backpacking trip with one close friend, communicating and making decisions occur naturally as you already have a relationship established and know each other's strengths and weakness. As the size of a group increases, not only do the logistics increase, but so do the complexities of communicating and making decisions. Having a designated "leader" can aid in a number of ways during a backcountry trip, such as securing the necessary permits, organizing what to bring, and planning the daily activities. The leader's role will be dependent on his skills and those of the rest of the group. If the leader is much more experienced than the rest of the group, a directive leadership style could be the most effective, whereas in a group of similarly skilled participants, a consensus style might be best for decision making. Establishing open communication within a group of backcountry travelers is important, so that everyone feels like their thoughts and concerns have a chance to be heard. A group of outdoor enthusiasts usually has considerable knowledge and experiences that can make a trip in the wilderness a safe and fun experience. The challenge is utilizing all of the group's attributes so everyone feels appreciated and invested in the experience.

The larger the group, the more you have to work together to accomplish your goals.

Chapter Two

Extreme Temperatures

As humans our normal core body temperature averages 98.6 degrees Fahrenheit. Even a few degrees above or below that normal level causes extreme stress on our bodies. As a result, we have many physiological reactions to deal with changes in the temperature. Traveling in the backcountry often places us in challenging climatic conditions and increases the risk of cold (hypothermia) and heat (hyperthermia) related injuries.

HAZARD: HOT ENVIRONMENTS

Three factors affect hikers in hot environments: temperature, humidity, and direct solar radiation. In response, your body uses several mechanisms to stay comfortable in hot conditions. When your muscles contract while you are hiking, they generate heat. To get rid of excess heat, blood flow to the vessels in the skin increases, causing a red or flushed look when exercising hard. As the outside temperature increases, getting closer to our body's core temperature of 98 degrees, this method of getting rid of extra heat is less effective. Another physiological response is sweating. In dry environments our sweat evaporates, cooling the surface of the skin. In climates with high humidity, sweat does not evaporate, leaving you feeling hot

Wearing a hat and sunscreen and covering up will help you stay cooler and avoid sunburn.

and damp. This factor helps explain why you feel hotter and more uncomfortable hiking in the Florida Everglades than in the Grand Canyon, even if the ambient air temperature is the same in both locations.

Along with losing water through sweat, we also lose water through breathing and urinating, so staying hydrated is very important in hot environments. The body can process up to one quart of water per hour during intense exercise or hot conditions, so drink up during your backcountry adventures.

In addition, the ambient air temperature of any environment can be further increased by the sun's solar radiation. Reducing your level of exertion, the amount of time you spend in the direct sunlight, and covering exposed skin when you travel will make you feel cooler.

Steps to Avoid Heat Injuries

» Choose an appropriate time of year. Visit
the desert during cooler seasons, when
temperatures are lower and water sources may
be more available. During hot seasons plan
to do most of your travel in the early morning
when the temperatures are lowest.

» Cover up. The ambient air temperature of
any environment can be further increased
by the sun's solar radiation. Wearing loose
fitting, lightweight, breathable clothing, a
wide brimmed hat and even gloves to cover
exposed skin will actually make you feel cooler

Heat Injuries		
	Symptom	Treatment
Heat Exhaustion	Weakness, headache, nausea, thirst	Put in shade, hydrate, rest
Heat Stroke	Similar to heat exhaustion plus body temperature is above 104 degrees Fahrenheit.	Immediate aggressive cooling (such as pouring cold water on the victim) to bring body temperature down, and then treat.

Desert Environments

The fantastic geological features, as well as the unique plant and animal species found in many deserts, make them appealing destinations for hikers. Deserts are defined as areas of land that receive less than ten inches of precipitation a year. In the United States there are over 350,000 square miles of desert habitat. The low rainfall and high temperatures of this harsh climate require visitors to plan ahead and use caution when traveling in the desert backcountry.

The desert can be a dangerous place for the unprepared.

and reduce the risk of sunburn. Also, less water evaporates from covered skin than from exposed skin, reducing dehydration. Apply waterproof sunblock to exposed skin.

» Protect your eyes. Sunglasses will reduce the chance of your corneas getting burned by the sun's ultraviolet rays and developing "snow blindness."

» Create your own shade. Hike with a lightweight umbrella.

» Stay hydrated. Carry enough water with you to safely navigate between known water sources. Do not rely on unknown springs or tanks listed on a map as they may only contain water during wet periods of the year. Using a hydration system such as a water bladder and attached drinking tube allows for constant intake of fluids while on the move.

» Remember to eat. Ingest enough calories to have energy for the day's activities and to maintain adequate electrolyte balance within your body. Hyponatremia is a condition in which there is not enough salt (sodium) in the body and this can quickly affect muscle, nerve, and even brain function, causing cramps, nausea, and a reduced level of consciousness. Eating a small amount of salty snacks will keep your electrolytes at proper levels. Take care of your feet: Hikers' feet often swell up in hot temperatures, and choosing well-fitting footwear that is both breathable and protective is important. In addition, low-cut gaiters can prevent sand and small pebbles from getting into your shoes and causing hot spots or blisters.

» Watch out for other desert dwellers. The harsh climatic conditions and relative open terrain of the desert have caused the plants and animals that live there to develop unique defenses to survive. Many plants have thorns and spines, and a number of arachnids (spiders and scorpions) and reptiles are poisonous.

HAZARD: COLD ENVIRONMENTS

When most novice backcountry users think about dealing with the cold, they often think about weather conditions typically encountered during the winter season. However, experienced hikers realize cold, "winter-like" conditions can be encountered during any season. Wilderness travel in mountainous regions can have an extreme range of temperatures dependent on the elevation. For every 1,000 feet gained in elevation, the temperature decreases by 3.5 degrees Fahrenheit. The elevation gain of the popular Keyhole Trail to the top of Longs Peak in Colorado is close to 5,000 feet, and 60-degree temperatures

Dealing with cold challenges every group.

encountered in the parking lot will plummet to the low 40s by the time you reach the summit—and that does not take into account the potential windchill effect.

People have a wide range of metabolisms and varying tolerances for cold conditions, but understanding how we lose heat to the environment is crucial in terms of outfitting ourselves in cold backcountry conditions. As we mentioned in the previous section, we generate heat by moving our muscles and other basic metabolic processes. This means that while hiking, especially carrying a heavy backpack, it is relatively easy to stay warm as long as you have been ingesting enough food and water.

Cold hazards often manifest themselves when you run out of energy or after you have stopped for the day. Two heat transfer mechanisms, conduction and convection, can quickly channel away body heat. We lose heat by conduction from direct contact with a cold surface through the soles of our boots, while standing in snow, or when sitting or sleeping on the ground. Convection is the loss of heat when the warm air next to your skin is displaced by cold air, often by wind, in the outdoor environment.

Getting out of the rain and drinking hot liquids will help prevent hypothermia.

Steps to Avoid Cold Injuries

» Layer up. Having several lightweight layers
    that can be worn together will allow you
    to fine-tune your clothing system to match
    the outside temperature conditions. The
    old saying "If you are cold put on a hat"
    makes sense, but in reality, any skin that is

Types of Cold Injuries		
	Symptom	Treatment
Hypothermia	Headache, irritability, loss of coordination caused by lowering of the core temperature	Rewarm with activity, liquids
Frostbite	Partially or fully frozen skin or appendages that are cold, hard, often with waxy or white-looking skin, itchiness, pain when rewarmed	Rewarm; technique depends on the severity. Don't allow to refreeze.
Immersion or Trench Foot	Loss of blood flow and nerve damage as the result of feet being wet and cool; results in red, swollen, numb toes and feet	Dry and rewarm

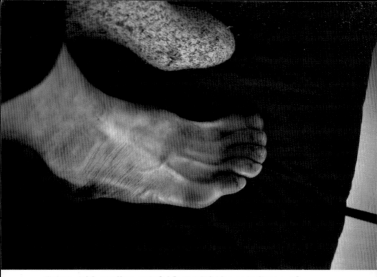

Damp, cold, swollen, painful feet might be an indicator of trench foot.

exposed will lose heat at the same rate, so cover up.

» Don't sweat it. Try and anticipate how your metabolism will respond to a specific outdoor activity and wear just enough clothing to keep yourself warm without sweating. In the desert environment, sweating was our friend, but in cold conditions evaporative cooling can quickly lower your core temperature. In addition, having sweat-soaked clothes against your skin will conduct additional heat away from your body. Choose fast-drying synthetic or wool blends instead of cotton base layers.

» Sleep warm. A 40-below-zero bag will do little to keep you warm during a frigid night unless you have an adequate sleeping pad to insulate you from the cold ground. Bringing an extra pair of dry socks that are worn only when you are sleeping will keep your toes toasty at night. For those people who sleep cold, putting a hot water bottle and having a snack in your sleeping bag are two ways to stay warm through the night.

» Remember that calories equal warmth. The caloric demands during a winter camping trip are huge and it is not the time to start a diet! During the day choose foods high in complex carbohydrates that digest at a medium rate, keeping your energy at a constant, well-fueled level. For the evening meal, add fats or proteins that digest slower and will help keep you warm throughout the night.

» Avoid dehydration. Unlike hot environments where you will often be thirsty, the urge to drink liquids can be reduced in a cold environment. Bringing a lightweight thermos to carry hot drinks during the day can increase your fluid intake.

Chapter Three

Precipitation

The term precipitation is used to describe rain, snow, sleet, hail, and graupel. Each of these forms of precipitation has its own associated hazards. A blizzard can cause limited visibility, which can make navigation challenging; becoming soaked by a cold rainstorm can lead to hypothermia; and heavy hail can damage your tent. Choosing the right equipment and appropriate hiking and camping techniques is essential for improving your comfort and safety in wet conditions.

HAZARD: RAIN AND SNOW

For backcountry users the two most important types of precipitation are rain and snow. The impact of a rainstorm or snow event on a wilderness experience varies depending on the temperature. For example, a three-day hike on the island of Kauai in steady rain with the temperature never dipping below 90 degrees Fahrenheit is much different than three days of rain in Denali National Park in 40 degree Fahrenheit conditions, which is also different than a long weekend spent winter camping in 5 degree Fahrenheit temperatures during a snowstorm in Rocky Mountain National Park. In Kauai, even if all of your gear gets soaked, there is no danger of any cold-related injury.

High-quality rain gear, including rain hats and pack covers, will help hikers deal with rainy conditions. A good attitude doesn't hurt either.

However, during a cold rainstorm in Denali, there is a real threat of both hypothermia and trench foot, and in the Rocky Mountains during the winter, you have the added threat of frostbite.

Obviously, the gear needed for each trip will be drastically different and so will hiking and packing techniques. Prior research into what average temperatures and precipitation you can expect will go a long way in helping you plan for your outdoor adventure.

Techniques for Coping with Precipitation in the Backcountry

» Keep your gear dry. Some experienced hikers swear by lining the inside of their backpack with a heavy duty trash compactor bag to waterproof their pack and stuffing everything inside. Other people have good luck using a commercially made pack cover. Still other backcountry users will line their sleeping bag stuff sack and other stuff sacks they want to keep dry with plastic bags and let other items like cookware, food, and the shelter get wet. Whatever technique you decide to use, your sleeping bag and extra clothes should be dry when you arrive at camp.

» Choose the right clothing system. For dealing with hiking in cold, wet conditions on overnight trips, there are two main schools of thought. The first is not to worry about getting wet and to rely on heat generated by the act of hiking to keep you warm. Then when you arrive in camp you quickly change into dry clothes and full rain gear. This techniques works as long as the temperature is not too cold. The second technique involves wearing appropriate layers to try to stay dry during the hike. The challenge with this technique is not overheating and soaking your clothes in sweat. Modern outerwear has a wide continuum of waterproof/breathable levels and it is now possible to find clothing that matches almost any condition. Finally, bring adequate gloves and mittens to keep your hands warm and dry. Wet, cold, nonfunctioning fingers will limit your ability to change layers, set up a shelter, light your stove, and perform other essential cold weather travel skills.

» Dry out your wet clothing. Regardless of the hiking clothing system you choose, chances are you will end up with some wet clothes during extended rainy periods. Some hikers just pile up their wet clothes in the vestibule of the tent and change back into them before starting to hike the next morning. Another technique is to dry out some of your wet clothing while you sleep. Your body continually pumps out heat and by placing damp clothing inside your sleeping bag you can dry it out during the course of the night. A synthetic sleeping bag is essential for this technique and trying to dry too many wet clothes will leave both you and your clothes soggy and cold in the morning, so some experimentation is required to figure out your own human clothes drier capacity.

» Compare down versus synthetic insulating gear. The benefit of down is that it is extremely lightweight and compresses well for packing when compared to synthetic insulation. However, when down gets wet it clumps up, losing almost all of its insulation value, while synthetic retains its insulating capacity even when wet. Your decision on what type of sleeping bag or puffy jacket you will use should be based on the weather conditions, where you are going, and how careful you are about keeping things dry.

» Compare tents versus snow shelters when winter camping. Some backcountry travelers use snow shelters instead of tents when winter camping. Snow shelters can be very warm compared to the outside temperatures, but require considerable work to build, which can cause clothing to get soaked from snow and sweat. If you plan to build a snow shelter, practice in a benign environment (like the backyard) before trusting your life to one in the backcountry.

Chapter Four
Wind

Hurricanes, tornadoes, and dust storms are major meteorological events that have associated high winds. Hurricanes are formed by warm air rising off the surface of the ocean and the action of other wind events such as thunderstorms. As the warm air rises into the atmosphere, it creates a vacuum, which in turn sucks in more air and energy into the tropical storm, creating high winds. When the wind speeds reach over 74 miles per hour, the storm is classified as a hurricane. Tornadoes are often part of hurricanes, but can also form independently on land as well as over the ocean. Dust storms occur when high winds pass over arid land and pick up small sand particles, carrying them suspended in the atmosphere.

Lenticular clouds are striking but indicate high winds and incoming weather.

HAZARD: EXTREME WIND

The highest documented surface wind speed, 231 miles per hour, was recorded at the weather station on the summit of Mount Washington in 1934. However, even mild wind events can affect hikers in several ways. First, hiking in windy conditions takes more energy, and strong wind gusts can cause you to lose your balance; add a large pack that can catch the wind like a sail and the difficulty of walking is increased dramatically. Second, in cold climates wind speed can cause a variety of cold injuries. If the wind is blowing at 15 miles per hour and the outside temperature is 0 degrees Fahrenheit, the windchill factor makes it feel like it is −20 degrees Fahrenheit. Exposed skin can freeze within 30 minutes under these conditions. Third, visibility is often decreased due to blowing snow or sand, making navigation challenging and increasing the likelihood of getting lost.

In exposed campsites, use extra guylines and rocks to secure your tent.

Steps for Dealing with Windy Conditions

» Do your research. Check weather data to see the likelihood of wind events as well as the current conditions in the backcountry area you will be visiting.

» Plan your travel day accordingly. In many locations, wind speed tends to increase during the day, so plan on doing the bulk of your hiking when wind speeds are the lowest.

» Cover up. Wear windproof clothing to reduce heat loss and prevent frostbite. In blizzard conditions, goggles, hoods, scarfs, and neck gaiters will prevent snow from getting in your eyes, ears, nose, and mouth. Finally, in sandy conditions, wear prescription glasses instead of contacts to reduce eye irritation.

» Choose your campsite wisely. Avoid camping in exposed windy locations. Look for shelter created by trees, boulders, and other natural wind blocks, but watch out for dead branches or trees that could blow down on your tent. Orient your tent with the door facing toward the prevailing wind direction. Learn how to secure your tent to the ground using cord, tent stakes, rocks, and other anchors. If you are camping in snow, build wind walls to protect your tent or excavate a snow shelter.

» Keep your equipment organized. At camp make sure to secure all of your gear either

Snow block walls make great wind walls to shelter your tent from high winds.

inside your tent or in your pack, so that it does not blow away or get buried by snow and become lost while you sleep.

Follow these special precautions for dealing with hurricanes, tornadoes, and dust storms: Move away from dangers such as dead limbs or dead trees in a forest. Take shelter in caves, rock overhangs, in between large boulders. If you are caught in the open, look for a low point such as a trench or ditch and lie as flat as possible in these features. Goggles and bandannas will prevent sand and other debris from getting in your eyes, ears, nose, and mouth. Be aware of other hazards associated with wind events. Hurricanes can also produce torrential rains, ocean storm surges, and flash flooding, so be aware of these dangers and how they relate to your location.

Chapter Five
Lightning

Lightning is a powerful natural phenomenon that has evoked curiosity and fear for thousands of years. Lightning is a gigantic discharge of electrostatic energy. This is the same kind of electricity that can shock you when you touch a doorknob after walking across a carpet. Lightning can occur between clouds and the ground, other clouds, or within a cloud.

HAZARD: LIGHTNING STRIKE

Scientists still do not fully understand how lightning forms, but they do know the conditions needed for lightning to occur. Wind, humidity, change in atmospheric pressure, and the friction between ice particles within a cloud combine to produce a separation of positive and negative charges creating lightning. Lightning can travel at speeds over 140,000 miles per hour and reach temperatures of over 50,000 degrees Fahrenheit. The associated thunder we hear is the result of rapidly expanding gases caused by the lightning bolt. Despite the incredible forces generated by lightning and its frequent occurrence, fewer than 75 people are killed by lightning each year in the United States.

Lightning often strikes the high locations that backpackers and climbers frequent.

Tips for Avoiding Lightning Strikes

» Plan activities to avoid being in high-risk areas. If you are climbing a peak or crossing a high pass or plateau, time your travel so that you are not in a high, exposed area during prime lightning time (typically noon or later).

» Use the sound of thunder to help predict lightning strikes. You can hear thunder up to 10 miles away and you should modify your travel plans as soon as you hear it. To further estimate how close lightning is to your location, count

the seconds from when you see a lightning strike to the time you hear the associated thunder and divide by 5. This gives you a rough estimation of how many miles away the storm is.

» Avoid dangerous locations. While seeking shelter inside a building or a vehicle provides shelter from lightning strikes in the frontcountry, in the backcountry, we are more vulnerable and try to avoid being in high and exposed places. Avoid mountaintops, exposed ridges, and wide-open flat ground. In addition, stay clear of individual long or tall objects such as lone trees or fence rows that can attract lightning. Also, do not stand in the mouth of a cave or rock overhang where your body can act like a spark plug, bridging the gap and allowing electrical current to travel in the most direct path—through you.

» Get into a safe lightning position. Sometimes it impossible to move to a safe location and you must wait out a storm. To avoid the effects of ground current and direct lightning strikes, crouch on a sleeping pad with your feet together and simply wait out the storm. Get away from long objects such as tent poles and ice axes that attract lightning.

Chapter Six

Natural Disasters

Hollywood regularly produces blockbuster movies with plots focused around natural disasters. Why? Because people are fascinated by the raw power of nature and the fact that, despite all of mankind's technological advances, we still cannot predict and control these forces. While natural disasters affect relatively few backcountry travelers, researching the likelihood of an event and knowing what to do if a disaster occurs are good ideas.

HAZARD: VOLCANOES AND EARTHQUAKES

Volcanoes and earthquakes are geological events characterized by the release of energy in the Earth's crust. There are over 500 active volcanoes in the world today. The locations of volcanoes and the relative likelihood of dangerous eruptions occurring in these regions are well documented—avoiding areas where an active volcano might erupt is the best way to avoid this hazard. When visiting a nonerupting volcano, don't get too close to the crater rim because the edges can give way unexpectedly. The craters can also have vents that release potential harmful gasses; avoid breathing such fumes.

Earthquakes, on the other hand, are much more unpredictable in terms of where and when they might take place. When they do occur, the specific hazards that backcountry travelers need to be aware of include falling branches and trees, sinkholes, snow avalanches, landslides, rockfall, and resulting tsunamis.

HAZARD: FOREST FIRES

Over a million acres of land are burned as the result of forest fires each year, and most of this is public land. While about 10 percent of the forest fires are started by natural causes such as lightning, the rest are started on purpose or by accident by people.

Forest fires are hazards in and of themselves, but they also leave behind standing dead trees long after the fire is out. The standing dead trees are more likely to be blown over by wind than live trees are, and they represent an additional hazard to backcountry travelers.

Some public lands, like Yellowstone National Park, have a "let burn" policy. In 1988, 793,880 acres or 36 percent of the park burned.

If you are on an extended backpacking trip, you might not have any knowledge of a forest fire that has ignited since you left the trailhead.

Tips for Staying Safe during a Forest Fire

» Evacuate the area as soon as you see smoke.

» Cross a fire break (e.g., road or river) to the other side away from the fire.

» If possible, head toward large areas that do not have vegetation, such as a boulder field or lake. The larger the area, the less smoke you'll have to inhale.

» Don't descend into a valley where a fire is burning—the more barriers between you and the fire, the safer you'll be.

» If a fire overtakes you, find some exposed ground and try to cover yourself with soil and lie face down until the fire passes over you.

» If the fire has burned out, be careful of branches still burning overhead and dead trees weakened by the fire that may fall.

Chapter Seven
Steep and Challenging Terrain

Hikers not only face challenges due to the angle of a route, but also due to what the "trail" medium is composed of. Even established hiking trails can present obstacles such as loose gravel, rocks, boulders, roots, and downed trees to navigate through. Leaves, rain, snow, and ice produced by changing seasons and inclement weather can further complicate your foot travel. Off-trail hiking can add bushwhacking, boulder fields, rock slabs, snow slopes, and even glaciers into the mix.

HAZARD: SCREE, TALUS, BOULDERS, AND SMALL CLIFFS

The terms scree, talus, and boulders all refer to rocks and are sometimes used interchangeably, but they can be differentiated by their size and how they are formed. Scree and talus slopes are formed when chunks of rock cleave off a cliff due to some types

Scree slopes are often loose and unstable.

of physical weathering processes, often freeze-thaw, and fall onto a slope below a cliff. The small rocks, roughly smaller than a football, are often called scree and the larger rocks are called talus. Scree and talus pile up at the steepest possible angle until gravity or additional accumulation of eroding rocks push the scree farther down the slope. As a result, scree fields are often very unstable and challenging to walk through. Established trails through this type of terrain tend to be traverses or low-angle diagonals up a slope. Attempting to hike straight up a scree slope is often an exercise in futility, as you will find yourself sliding one step back for nearly every step upward. On certain scree slopes that are composed of small golf ball-to-baseball-size rocks, hikers can "scree ski" by doing a controlled slide on their feet down the slope. Before you start "skiing," make sure no one is below you to get hit by tumbling rocks and you do not go too fast and lose control, as a fall into a rock slope is much more painful than on a snow slope.

Navigating through boulder fields can be time consuming, but rushing can make them even more hazardous.

The "butt scooch" is a good technique for getting down large boulders.

Some boulder fields are formed by glacial activity. As glaciers recede, the sand, pebbles, rocks, and boulders trapped within the ice melt out and are left behind. In the continental United States, many of the glacial boulder fields were laid down at the end of the last ice age over 10,000 years ago. As a result, the individual boulders are fairly stable. Often, boulders of similar weight will be deposited in the same location. For a hiker this is either a blessing or a curse depending on the size of the boulders and steepness of the terrain. Boulders smaller than a microwave can be "tippy," and careful attention needs to be focused on where you place your feet, while boulders larger than a truck are often spaced farther apart and climbing them takes more time and energy especially while wearing a backpack.

Scrambling up a steep rock step requires good footwork.

Sometimes during off-trail hiking, the terrain to get from point A to point B on a topographic map looks much different than the terrain in real life. If the contour intervals on a map are set to 40 feet, you may be surprised to find a 39-foot rock cliff in front of you that did not show up on the map. Scrambling up steep rocky slopes can sometimes be much faster than traveling around an obstacle, but to do it safely hikers should consider the following questions. One: If I slip, can I stop myself and how far will I fall? Two: If my route does not go, can I safely climb back down?

HAZARD: ROCKFALL

Rockfall can be generated by many different things, including seasonal and daily freeze-thaw cycles, wind, heavy rain, earthquakes, wild and domestic animals, people in your group, and other parties ahead of (or above) you.

Tips for Avoiding Rockfall

Whenever you travel through steep terrain, observe the base of a cliff or slope and look for recent signs of rockfall. If there are other people above you, consider choosing a different route or waiting in a safe zone until they have moved through the terrain. When traveling as a group through loose scree or talus, stick close together so if a rock is dislodged, it will not have time to generate a lot of force as it rolls toward someone else in your party.

Tips for Safe Navigation of Rocky Terrain

» Travel through tough terrain at the beginning of the day while you are fresh and take frequent rest breaks.

» Choose a route based on the ability of the weakest member of your group.

» If the terrain looks challenging, consider scouting it without packs to make sure your route will work.

» Stay mentally focused and save the sightseeing for the rest breaks. One misstep can result in a sprained ankle, broken leg, or worse.

» Trekking poles can reduce trauma to your joints and aid in balance, especially on descents, but they can also get in the way when you need to use both hands.

» Choose footwear that gives you support but is flexible enough to allow you to "feel" the rocks and boulders.

» When climbing up or down large boulders or short vertical steps, consider passing the packs through the difficult section and or "spotting" people as they climb, so you are in a ready position to stop a fall and prevent injury.

» Rain can make boulders—and especially lichen growing on the boulders—very slippery. Careful foot placement helps.

» If you do dislodge a rock, yell "ROCK!" so everyone knows of the hazard potentially coming at them.

HAZARD: STEEP SNOW AND ICE

While steep snow and ice is considered the domain of mountaineers, general hikers and backcountry users can find themselves in this environment and should be aware of the common hazards associated with these types of terrain. Avalanches are a serious danger on steep snow slopes and will be covered in the next section.

The biggest hazard in both steep snow and ice travel is falling on the slope. More specifically, it is the inability to stop or arrest your fall once it occurs. While there are technical rope systems you can learn to protect a fall, they are beyond the scope of this book. Instead, we will examine techniques and precautions you can use to safely move through steep snow and ice.

Snow is an incredibly variable medium. Unlike a steep gravel trail, where the conditions remain the same throughout the day and night, a snow slope can change dramatically in a twenty-four-hour period. You might use snowshoes, crampons, or light hiking boots to climb the same steep snow slope depending on the conditions. Knowing the appropriate ascension technique to be safe and efficient is a big part of climbing snow and ice slopes. There are certainly dangers while climbing up a slope, but most accidents occur on the way down. Most novices recognize the dire consequences of a fall on a steep cliff without a rope, but a slip on a 35-degree snow slope seems much less serious. However, snow and ice has very little friction and a person can quickly rocket out of control. Beginner backcountry travelers should stick to terrain that they will not be likely to fall on. If for some reason you do slip, you should have the skills to be able to stop (arrest) the fall before it gets out of control.

Equipment for Negotiating Steep Snow and Ice

The ice axe is the iconic image of mountaineering and many people believe simply purchasing an ice axe and carrying it in their hands will keep them safe in the mountains. However, without the necessary skill and training, an ice axe is at best something that gets dropped in a fall on a steep slope; at worst it might become impaled in its owner. Ice axe techniques, like the self-arrest, should be mastered in a safe environment with proper instruction before being used to save your life. A better option for novices is to stick to moderately angled slopes with less exposure and use trekking poles, which are a more intuitive way to help with balance and short slips.

Crampons are another climbing tool that is often misused. The two points sticking out of the front of the crampons are used for climbing steep ice, and putting your weight on these "front points" stresses your calf muscles. The points on the bottom of the crampons are better used for climbing moderately steep snow and ice. This flat-footed crampon technique uses the larger quadriceps muscle of the leg and conserves energy. The main reason beginners fall when using crampons has nothing to do with the frozen terrain they are climbing, but is instead often the result of mistakenly catching their pants leg or gaiter with their crampon points. Another reason people fall while wearing crampons is because wet snow "balls up" on the bottom of the crampons and makes footing difficult. Use your ice axe or trekking poles to periodically tap the sides of your crampons to dislodge the snow, or better yet, remove your crampons, as the snow is soft enough that you probably do not need them.

Ascending Techniques for Steep Snow and Ice

» Kicking steps: While maintaining a diagonal direction up a moderately soft snow slope, slice your boots (without crampons) into the snow, creating a level platform for each foot. The next person up the track will walk directly in your tracks and try to improve the steps.

Cutting switchbacks saves energy versus climbing straight up a steep slope.

» Front pointing: On steep snow or ice, kick the toes of your boots with or without crampons into the snow and travel directly up the slope. Try to lower your heels to relax your calves.

Descending Techniques for Steep Snow and Ice

» The plunge step: In moderately soft snow, face away from the slope, aggressively kick your heels into the snow, and walk directly down the slope. If the snow is harder, you can always face the slope and "front point" down, being careful not to catch a point and flip over backwards.

"Plunge stepping" down a steep slope on soft snow can make for a quick descent.

Glissading offers a fast, fun way down, but don't let the slide get out of control. Learn self-arrest techniques with the ice axe.

» Glissading: This is a great technique to quickly descend a snow slope. It can be done from a standing, crouching, or seated position. First check to make sure there is not a sheer cliff or other hazard at the bottom of the slope. Second, take your crampons off, as the points can catch in the snow and break your ankle or lower leg. Start off by slowly sliding down the slope. You can check your speed by digging your heels into the snow while in the seated position. If you feel you cannot slow down, use your ice axe to self-arrest. If you do not know how to self-arrest, quickly flip onto your stomach and dig into the snow with your elbows or hands while simultaneously kicking the toes of both boots into the snow to stop.

HAZARD: AVALANCHES

The word *avalanche* originated in Switzerland and literally means a mass of falling snow. Avalanches can be caused by natural or human triggers. There are also several factors that can contribute to an avalanche, such as the steepness of a slope (30–45 degrees is the most common), weather, temperature, which direction the slope faces, wind direction, shape, and composition of the terrain under the snow pack. Some of these factors, including wind direction, temperature, and snow accumulation, can change daily or hourly.

There are three main types of avalanches: loose snow, slab, and wet snow avalanches. Loose snow avalanches are caused when newly fallen snow, with less density, accumulates on steeper slopes and sloughs from a narrow point, widening as it travels down the slope, often resembling a tear drop shape. A slab avalanche occurs when a well-bonded layer of snow within the snow pack is released suddenly down a slope, usually as the result of another weak layer collapsing. Slab avalanches fracture very quickly and can contain huge amounts of snow. These avalanches account for the vast majority of avalanche fatalities. The third type of avalanche is called a wet snow avalanche and is caused by the snow pack becoming saturated with water. Like the loose snow avalanches, these often begin from a point and spread out down the slope. The water within the snow acts as a lubricant, and as a result, these avalanches can move on very shallow angled snow slopes.

Carrying avalanche rescue tools like an avalanche transceiver is important when you head into the backcountry in winter.

Steps for Staying Safe in Avalanche Terrain

>> Learning how to interpret the snow pack and accurately predict how safe or dangerous a particular slope is takes time and experience under the tutelage of experts.

» Stay on slopes less than 25 degrees.

» Look for signs of previous avalanche activity.

» Ridges or buttresses are safer choices for travel than convex slopes or gullies where the tension fractures can cause avalanches.

» Stay near snow pack anchors, such as dense stands of trees and rock outcroppings.

» Know the weather history of the snow pack.

» Wear an avalanche transceiver and know how to search for a buried victim with it.

» In questionable terrain, travel one at a time across a suspect slope. If you are caught in an avalanche, try to get rid of skis, snowshoes, and other items that might drag you down, and swim or roll to the side of the slide path. Those not caught should watch and take note of where the victim was last seen; begin searching from that point down and look for other signs of the victim, such as ski poles, gloves, packs, etc.

HAZARD: LANDSLIDES

Landslides or mudslides occur when rocks, soil, and other debris become saturated with water from snow melt, heavy rainfall or ground water and slide down a steep slope. Like snow avalanches, landslides can occur without warning, travel at a high rate of speed, and be deadly, crushing and burying everything in their path.

Events that can trigger or increase the likelihood of landslides include storms, earthquakes, volcanic eruptions, fire, freezing and thawing cycles and slopes becoming steeper as the result of erosion or human modification. Visible debris piles from previous landslides, a history of landslide in the area through which you are traveling, and recent climatic conditions are your best resources in terms of predicting new landslides.

HAZARD: GLACIERS

Glaciers are semi-permanent masses of ice and snow that move over land. Ten percent of the Earth's surface is covered with glaciers. Glaciers are often formed in the mountains when more snow accumulates in the winter season than melts in the summer. As snow and ice amasses, a glacial "river" begins to flow down the mountain under the force of gravity. This process is very slow, often just a few feet a year. The glacial river scours the underlying bedrock, creating large, U-shaped

On late-season glaciers that haven't received recent snowfall, you can often—but not always—see the crevasses.

valleys. Glaciers are also affected by the steepness of the terrain and curvature of the land. The glacier bends and cracks as it moves down the mountain. These cracks are called crevasses. One way to imagine how crevasses are formed is to hold a candy bar like a Snickers bar in your hand and then bend it at a sharp angle. The candy bar will at first flex, and then cracks will appear on the outside of the bend. If you bend it back the other way, the cracks will close and new ones will form on the opposite side. A glacier essentially behaves like a really long Snickers bar. It bends and cracks, creating crevasses as it works it way down the mountain.

The area of the glacier, usually high in the mountains, where cold temperatures allow snow and ice to build up, is called the zone of accumulation. The lower portion of the glacier, where it is warmer and the ice and snow are constantly melting, is called the zone of ablation. The transition between these two regions is often called the firn zone, an important location in terms of traveling through glacial terrain. Above the firn zone crevasses are often covered by snow. This snow depth can vary from dozens of feet to a few inches thick, making snow bridges above crevasses extremely dangerous. Route finding through snow-covered glacial terrain is challenging, and safety systems such as roped travel and knowledge of rescue techniques is essential above the firn zone.

Below the firn zone the snow has often melted, exposing the bare ice of the glacier. Being able to see the potential hazards will allow you to plan a safe route across low-angled sections of a glacier. If the crevasses are narrow, they can simply be stepped

Leaping across a crevasse can have serious consequences if you don't make it to the other side. Roping up would add a significant margin of safety to this maneuver.

over; if they are wide, they can be circumvented. When a glacier moves through steep terrain, large chunks of ice called seracs can break off from the main ice and tumble down a slope. The likelihood and timing of serac fall is impossible to predict, so the best way to deal with this type of hazard is to avoid it by keeping a safe distance and going around it.

Water created by the melting glaciers can also create hazards. On large glaciers, streams and even small rivers of meltwater can block progress. The meltwater can accumulate in low areas or be contained by an ice dam that can melt and rupture, causing a flood downstream. Water flowing down the surface of the ice can drain into deep cracks and further erode these cracks until they form dangerous vertical sinkholes called moulins.

Techniques for Traveling Safely on Glaciers

- » Do not travel above the firn zone unroped.
- » Be aware of changing conditions: Ice bridges that were solid and safe to cross in the morning might melt and collapse by evening.
- » Maintain a safe distance from hazards: Edges of crevasses and moulins can collapse without warning.
- » Look for dangers above you: Seracs and rockfall from glacial movement and freeze-thaw process can be extremely dangerous.

» Use appropriate safety equipment: Wear crampons when walking up steeper slopes of bare ice. Trekking poles are useful for maintaining balance while stepping across crevasses. An ice axe can be used to chop steps up a short slope when you are not wearing crampons or for support to pull over a short bulge.

HAZARD: HIGH ALTITUDE

High-altitude terrain is usually defined as areas above 10,000 feet. Backcountry users often notice they quickly get out of breath while hiking or climbing at or above this elevation. One common misconception is the air at higher elevations contains less oxygen. In fact the percentage of oxygen is relatively the same at all levels of the atmosphere. So why is it harder to breath at higher elevations? If you imagine the atmosphere as a giant ocean of air, at the surface of the Earth the weight or pressure of all the air above causes the air's molecules, including oxygen, to get pushed together. As you move up in elevation, there is less air pushing down (atmospheric pressure) and the molecules within the atmosphere move apart. As a result, at 10,000 feet each breath of air you take in has only 70 percent as much oxygen as at sea level. The reduced atmospheric pressure and the lower availability of oxygen in each breath at higher elevations are the main causes of altitude illness. While researchers are trying to determine why some people are physiologically more affected than others at high elevations, the signs, symptoms, and treatments of altitude illnesses have been well studied.

Acute Mountain Sickness (AMS)

The most common symptom of AMS is a headache, often caused by dehydration. It is much easier to get dehydrated at altitude; as the air becomes drier and as your breathing increases, so does the loss of water through respiration. Increased respiration also causes a host of compensating responses that further stress your body. Other signs and symptoms of AMS include nausea, lethargy, and loss of balance. For most people these symptoms will disappear over a short period of time. However, if they persist for several days or worsen, descent to a lower elevation is advisable. One drug, acetazolamide, can reduce the side effects of AMS and can help you with acclimatization, but is not a magic bullet.

High-Altitude Cerebral Edema (HACE)

HACE involves the swelling of a person's brain at altitude. Climbers often show signs of being confused, have blurred vision, and have trouble with basic motor functions such as walking. HACE is an immediate threat to life and descent is critical. The drug dexamethasone, which is a powerful steroid, has been shown to reduce the symptoms of HACE.

High-Altitude Pulmonary Edema (HAPE)

HAPE develops when the lung arteries develop excessive pressure in response to low oxygen, and the results are leaking of fluid into the lungs. Signs and symptoms of HAPE include all of those for severe AMS, as well as a cough, which may produce frothy or pink sputum, gurgling or rattling breaths, and tightness in the chest. A fast descent is the best treatment; the drug nifedipine has been shown to help with HAPE.

Tips on Dealing with the Effects of Altitude

- » Adapt to high altitudes slowly: When you get above 10,000 feet in elevation, do not attempt to gain more than 2,000 additional feet in elevation between camps.
- » Climb high, sleep low; use day hikes to help acclimatize.
- » Stay hydrated and well fed.
- » When altitude-related symptoms appear, descend before they get worse.

Chapter Eight

Water

Wading and swimming are very popular outdoor activities; however, the dangers of crossing water with a heavy pack—especially moving water—are often underestimated by hikers and backpackers. In Alaska's Denali National Park many backcountry users fixate on the risks associated with traveling through grizzly bear habitat, but in fact, hikers face a much deadlier hazard when attempting to cross the cold, glacial-fed streams and rivers.

Unbuckle your hipbelt and straps for tricky crossings so the pack doesn't drag you under if you fall.

HAZARD: MOVING WATER

Many established hiking trails have bridges that allow hikers to easily cross over streams and rivers. However, bridges can get washed away in floods and many wilderness trails do not have bridges. The backcountry traveler is left to her own devices in terms of figuring out the best way to cross a stream or river. As a result, crossing moving water is a major outdoor hazard that all backcountry travelers encounter at some point. Moving water by its nature is constantly changing and no two crossings are the same, which requires you to be proficient in a number of different crossing techniques.

Safely Crossing Rivers and Streams

Stream and river crossings can be divided into two main types: wet and dry crossings. Dry crossing involves using rocks, tree trunks, logs jams, and Tyroleans to get across rivers, hopefully keeping your feet dry in the process. Consider scouting a dry river crossing without packs to determine its difficulty and what the repercussions would be if you do fall into the water. Rock hopping across flat, closely spaced, featured rocks can be a fast and effective way to cross a river. However, if the rocks are covered with algae and far apart, it might be safer to simply wade rather than risk injury leaping between slippery rocks. Throwing sand on the surface of slick rocks or logs and using trekking poles to maintain balance are a

Wading across rivers can produce hypothermia.

couple of ways to make dry crossing easier. Log jams can be very unstable and great care should be used in determining the overall solidity of the mass of debris. A Tyrolean traverse is a section of rope or cable that is tensioned between two trees or boulders on opposite banks of a river, and onto which people attach themselves to cross above the water. Tyrolean traverses take time to set up, require a fair amount of technical equipment and rope skills, and require at least one person to initially cross the river to set the rope up on the opposite side. However, they are a useful crossing technique with a large group or if you have to cross the river several times.

Wet crossings involve getting in the water and wading or swimming from one bank to the other. When determining what type of crossing technique is best, outdoor travelers should look at the volume, speed, and depth of the water, and the type of sub-strate on the river bottom.

There are two basic types of wet crossings that are often used with a group of people. The first is the chain method, in which people face upstream, hold hands or lock arms, and step together across the river. The second method, the "eddy" technique, is used in deep, faster-moving water, where one person positions himself facing upstream and the rest of group stands behind the lead person in either a train or pyramid formation, and everyone walks in unison across the waterway. Once you determine the type of river crossing you will use, check out the entrance and exit points on the banks of the river. Determine what the hazards are downstream if you swim, where spotters should stand, and determine if you should cross now or wait until the water flow is less. To get ready for the crossing, remove long jackets or other clothing

Forming a human chain will increase your stability when crossing rivers and streams.

that will catch the water and act like sails. In addition, unless the riverbed is soft sand, you should wear some type of footwear to reduce injuries and to give you more support during the crossing.

Safety Tips for River Crossings

» Spend time to look at the potential hazards of each river crossing and remember you always have the option of not crossing the river.

» Waterproof important items in your pack.

» Don't look down into the water as swirling current might cause you to lose your balance.

» Have spotters downstream in case things go bad.

» Loosen your pack straps and consider undoing your hip buckle in case you fall in and need to quickly jettison your pack and swim to shore.

» If you do fall into the water, do not try to stand back up in the middle of the river, as your feet can become trapped between rock; instead, swim or float on your back toward shore using your legs to push away dangers in front of you.

HAZARD: FROZEN WATER

Frozen streams, rivers, and lakes can provide easy walking for the winter outdoor enthusiast, but falling through the ice can be fatal. For ice to support your weight, it should be at least three to four inches thick.

Crossing over frozen moving water on thin ice is very dangerous.

Stationary bodies of water tend to freeze more uni-
formly than rivers, but springs or streams flowing into
a pond or lake can cause thin spots. Pay attention to
recent weather conditions and look and listen for signs
of dangerous conditions such as cracking noises, open

Make sure the ice is at least 4 inches thick before crossing a frozen lake.

water, or wet patches of snow on the ice. Stay close enough to the shore to quickly be able to get out of the water if you break through the ice, as the cold and hypothermia will completely incapacitate you within a few minutes.

HAZARD: TIDAL AREAS

Coastal hiking and backpacking is a popular activity along the shoreline of many areas of the United States. Some trails and regions can only be accessed during low tide. Careful planning using a tide chart for reference is required to make sure you do not get stranded when the tide comes in. Ocean tides are affected by the gravitational pull of the moon, sun, and Earth. The highest high tides occur near the spring and fall equinox, when the Earth, moon, and sun are all in alignment. When choosing a campsite for the night, you should position yourself well above

Watch out for high tide during coastal hikes as your trail might be under water.

the high-tide mark, which can easily be identified by sticks, detached seaweed, and other buoyant debris piled up on the far edge of the shoreline or beach.

While high tides caused by the orientation of the moon, sun, and Earth can be planned for, there are other ocean conditions, such as storm surges and tsunamis, that are more random. The worst natural disaster in the United States occurred in 1900, when between 6,000 and 12,000 people were killed in Galveston, Texas, by a storm surge during a hurricane. A storm surge is caused when the high winds of a hurricane push down on the ocean's surface displacing water. This event, in combination with the low pressure created by the hurricane and an abnormally high tide, creates monster waves.

Tsunamis are huge waves of water created by a buckling or other disturbance in the sea floor, often the result of an earthquake. This buckling displaces large volumes of water and forms giant waves that travel for thousands of miles across the ocean, retaining enough lethal energy to destroy buildings, trees, wildlife, and people. Since the waves travel such far distances before striking land, they are difficult to anticipate because the area devastated by the tsunami might not even feel the initial earthquake. However, if you see the ocean receding at an unusually fast rate, it is a good indication that a big wave is on its way and you should immediately seek high ground.

Tight desert canyons like this can quickly fill with water during flash floods.

HAZARD: FLASH FLOODS

Flash floods can occur in any environment. They are caused by heavy rainfall, thunderstorms, and hurricanes, sometimes in conjunction with melting snow. In such conditions the soil and vegetation become completely saturated and the excess water pours into the surrounding drainages. The arid regions of the desert Southwest are especially susceptible to flash flooding in the summer season. Powerful thunderstorms can produce several inches of rain in a short period of time. The desert soil cannot absorb much of the rainfall, and the vast majority of the water runs immediately into creeks and other tributaries, tearing through canyons and ripping up vegetation and other debris at the bottom of the watershed.

For desert canyon hikers flash floods are a serious danger because there is often little warning before the flood. The thunderstorms that produce the flooding can be many miles away and the hikers might not even see clouds or feel rain before the water levels begin to rise.

Steps to Avoid Getting Caught in a Flash Flood

» When planning a canyon trip, study topographic maps of the region and identify sections of your route that are subject to flash floods; at the same time identify potential escape routes.

» Monitor the weather before you begin your backcountry adventure. Check the long-range forecast for the area you will be traveling through, as well as areas upstream of your location in the same watershed.

» Never camp in a wash at the bottom of a canyon, even though the often level open ground makes a comfortable, low-impact campsite.

» If you have to camp in a narrow canyon, look for the highest signs of flooding and camp well above that line.

» If you are caught in a canyon during a flash flood, do not try and outrun a wall of water. Instead, climb up above the water and wait for the storm to abate.

Chapter Nine

Vertebrates

One of the main reasons people venture into the backcountry is to enjoy the wilderness by observing the wildlife that lives there. However, the more you know about the behaviors and potential hazards associated with certain wild animals, the more enjoyable your experience in the wilds will be.

HAZARD: POTENTIALLY DANGEROUS VERTEBRATES

Bears

There are three species of bears living in the United States: polar bears, brown bears (grizzly and Kodiak), and black bears. Polar bears live in the northernmost regions of Alaska and Canada and are easily identi-

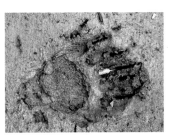

Look for signs of bear-like tracks in the mud or dug-up rocks and logs.

fied by their white color. They spend most of their lives on ice floes in the ocean and, although polar bears can be extremely dangerous, they are not often near people.

Bears will often hear or smell you before they see you. Making noise is a good way to avoid surprising a bear in the backcountry.

The historical range of the grizzly bear once extended along the western half of North America from Mexico to Alaska. Grizzly bears are common in Alaska and Canada but are considered endangered species in Washington, Idaho, Wyoming, and Montana. Black bears live throughout North America. In regions of the country where both bears live, it can be difficult to tell them apart. On average, grizzly bears are larger and black bears are darker in color. However, since both species vary in coloring and size, it is hard to identify them, especially at a distance. Grizzly bears often dig in the soil for food and have much longer claws and a pronounced hump on their back.

Black bears' claws are smaller, which makes them better tree climbers, and they do not have a hump on their back. In addition, grizzly bears have dish-shaped faces with a clear depression between the eyes and the end of the nose, whereas black bears have a straight profile and pointed snout.

Bear Safety Tips

The most likely and safest way to see a wild bear is while driving in your car. When hiking in the backcountry, it is best to avoid contact with any bear. Here are some ways to avoid hostile bear encounters:

» Travel in groups of four or more, as there is little data indicating that groups of this size or larger have problem encounters with bears.

» Do not surprise bears. Let them know you are approaching by making loud noises.

» Use designated food storage containers such as bear boxes and bear-proof food canisters. If these aren't available, hang your food from trees. Some areas provide "bear poles" to hang food from.

» Cook downwind and well away (100 yards) from your sleeping area.

» Carry pepper spray and have it instantly accessible as you hike. Bear encounters often happen quickly, and pepper spray won't do any good if it's stuffed away in your pack.

» If you do decide to carry a firearm, make sure you are legally allowed to do so in the area you are visiting and that you know how to use it effectively.

Bear attacks on people are very, very rare and occur either because the bear is provoked or the bear is looking for some food—either your food or, yes, you. A provoked bear can attack when it is startled, when it is defending its territory or food source, and especially when protecting its young. Bears will often exhibit a number of aggressive behaviors before an attack. These include swatting the ground with their paws, soft and/or loud vocalizations, and bluff charges. If you encounter a provoked bear, do not run or look the bear in the eye, but back slowly away from the bear. If a grizzly bear charges you and makes contact, play dead and hopefully the bear will stop the attack as you are no longer a threat. If the bear—most often a black bear, in this case—is stalking you as a source of food, it is best to be loud and aggressive and try to scare the bear away. If you are in a group, move closer together to appear larger. Many hikers carry pepper spray in a holster on their pack belt. Pepper spray has been proven effective in repelling aggressive bears.

Rabies

Rabies is a viral infection that affects the brain and nervous system of mammals. Once the neurological symptoms present themselves, the disease is almost always fatal. All mammals can contract rabies, and the virus is spread through bites from an infected animal. Rabies deaths in the United States are almost nonexistent, but worldwide the disease kills over 50,000 people annually. In the United States raccoons are the most common carriers of the virus, but bites from bats are the most likely reason for infections in humans. Anytime you are bitten by a wild animal, you should see a physician. The treatment for a suspected rabies infection is a series of three to five injections given in the arm. People who are working in or traveling to areas where rabies is common can get a series of pre-exposure vaccines.

Mountain Lions

Mountain lions, also called panthers and cougars, are the largest wild cat species living in North America. Adult males can weigh over 200 pounds. Mountain lions are found in a variety of habitats from deserts in Arizona to the coniferous forest of British Columbia. While their primary prey is deer, they are opportunists and will hunt and eat a variety of game. Mountain lions usually take down their prey by pouncing on the back of the intended victim. Cougar attacks are rare and, when they do occur, happen as the result of human development encroaching on mountain lion habitat. Small women and children traveling alone in the backcountry are most at risk for mountain lion attacks.

Mountain Lion Safety Tips

» As with bears, if you see a mountain lion in the wild, especially a female with young or a lion defending its prey, move away from the area.
» Do not run or crouch down when you see a cougar.
» Pick up small children and if you are in a group, bunch together and try and make yourself look bigger; then slowly back away from the mountain lion.
» Never stare into the eyes of a mountain lion.
» If a cougar comes toward you, act aggressive, yell, wave your arms, and throw rocks and branches at it.

Wolves and Coyotes

Like grizzly bears, wolves were once found in many states, but hunting brought them to near extinction in the continental United States. Gray wolves have been reintroduced to parts of Montana, Wyoming, Idaho, Minnesota, Wisconsin, and Michigan. An adult wolf can weigh up to 80 pounds and range in color from white to black. Wolves are pack animals and hunt large game such as deer, elk, and moose, but will also kill small mammals and birds. Wolves usually tend to avoid people and there have been only a handful of documented aggressive encounters; these have often been started as the result of people hiking with their dogs.

Coyotes are found in every state except Hawaii, which attests to their ability to thrive in a variety of ecosystems. Their size depends on the environment; in the desert coyotes rarely weigh more than 25 pounds, but in the Northeast where they often hunt deer, they can weigh as much as 70 pounds. They have adapted well to suburban environments by eating garbage, small dogs, and cats. Coyotes rarely attack humans; however, infants and small children should not be left unattended when in coyote habitat.

Coyotes are found throughout North America. They rarely bother humans, but small children should not be left unattended when coyotes are around.

Hooved Mammals (Ungulates)

There have been a few documented cases of people being attacked by moose, elk, mountain goats, and bison. Moose can be particularly aggressive during the fall when bulls go into the rut. As with most other animals, mothers with their calves can also be antagonistic. Almost all of these incidents occur when people try to approach too closely, often while trying to photograph the animals. If a moose is blocking the trail, don't try to scare it off. Instead, take the long way around, steering far clear of the animal so as not to disturb it.

Bull moose can be aggressive in the fall during mating season.

Elk are not usually aggressive toward people—but don't get too close!

Poisonous Snakes

Currently, there is at least one type of venomous snake found in every state in the United States, the exceptions being Maine, Alaska, and Hawaii. These snakes include the copperhead, cottonmouth, rattlesnake, and coral snake. Copperheads and cottonmouths are found in the East, coral snakes in the Southwest, and rattlesnakes throughout the continental United States. Coral snakes are black with alternating yellow and red bands. Copperheads, cottonmouths, and rattlesnakes have a variety of color patterns.

Despite the hype surrounding the dangers of snakes, fewer than a dozen people are killed each year by venomous snakes. When confronted by some type of danger, all snakes, even poisonous ones, will try and slither away instead of striking out at people.

A rattlesnake will warn you with its rattle if you get too close.

Rattlesnakes have rattles on the end of their tails, which they vibrate to warn people and other animals of their presence. The typical person to get bitten by a poisonous snake is a young male who has been trying to catch or pick it up. The toxins in snake venom cause severe pain, and the amount of poison depends on the species and size of the snake. Common effects of envenomation include nausea, swelling, weakness, and blurred vision. In addition, some toxins affect the central nervous system, causing paralysis and lung and heart failure. All victims of poisonous snake bites should be evacuated to a hospital as soon as possible to receive antivenin.

Treatment of Venomous Snake Bites

Note that some treatments that have been commonly accepted in the past are now known to be more harmful than helpful.

> » Try to determine the species of snake based on visual inspection.
>
> » Keep the person calm.
>
> » Remove rings, bracelets, etc., as the affected area will swell.
>
> » Keep the snake bite lower than the heart to reduce the flow of venom.
>
> » Evacuate quickly with as little movement as possible.

- » *Do not* make an incision in the skin with a knife or other cutting device.
- » *Do not* try and suck poison out with your mouth.
- » *Do not* apply a tourniquet.
- » *Do not* give any medication or alcohol.

HAZARD: ANIMALS THAT WANT YOUR FOOD

Why do animals want to eat the food we bring into the backcountry? The answer is energy conservation. It takes a bear much less energy to steal a sandwich out of a cooler than forage or hunt for its normal wild foods. But it's not just bears: Almost

Some backcountry campsites have secure metal food-storage containers to keep wildlife from getting your food.

Hanging your food is one option to reduce the chance that critters will get into it.

any species of wildlife can become habituated to human food. Coyotes, skunks, raccoons, marmots, squirrels, ringtail cats, and mice will seek out improperly stored food items. Even birds like crows and jays will scavenge food items. It is not uncommon to see ravens tearing into unattended stuff stacks filled with climbers' food at the 17,200-foot camp on Denali.

Besides causing you to lose your food supplies and ending your wilderness experience, there are several other reasons why human food and wildlife should not mix. If you feed wildlife or are careless with your food, you will cause the populations of animals to increase in a small area. An unnaturally high population leads to aggressive conflicts between animals and also spreads disease. A common saying in regard to feeding bears is, "A fed bear is a dead bear." Once a bear gets used to human food, it associates food with people and will harass people in the backcountry. The end result of this conflict is usually the bear being killed.

Even small rodents can chew through backpacks to get food.

Steps to Keep Critters from Raiding Your Food

» Use food storage lockers and carry animal-resistant containers.

» Bring a small amount of cord or rope and hang your food from a tree or boulder out of the reach of wildlife.

» For backcountry excursions with several participants and lots of food, small portable electric fences have been an effective alternative to hanging food.

» Pick up all food scraps dropped while eating or cooking and pack out all of your trash from the backcountry.

Chapter Ten

Arachnids, Insects, and Microscopic Creatures

This chapter deals with two main groups of invertebrate hazards: arthropods and one-celled microscopic creatures. Arthropods are a class of living creatures that have their skeleton on the outside rather than on the inside and include insects, spiders, and mites. There are between 4 to 6 million species of arthropods worldwide, and it is not surprising that a few of them can be problematic to backcountry travelers. Microscopic hazards include viruses, bacteria, and protozoans.

HAZARD: ARACHNIDS

Arachnids are a class of invertebrates that has over 100,000 identified species. Spiders, scorpions, and ticks are examples of arachnids. They can look similar to insects, but arachnids have eight legs instead of six and do not have wings or antennae.

Spiders

Did you know that every spider is poisonous? Yes, all spiders have some type of poison that they inject into their prey. Fortunately, very few spider bites actually are harmful to humans. Two species of spiders whose poison can be harmful are the black widow and brown recluse spider, both of which are found throughout North America.

Both the male and female black widow usually have a red hourglass shape on their abdomen. These spiders are not aggressive and bite only when provoked or protecting their eggs. The black widow bite is very painful. Other symptoms include headache, severe abdominal pain, and sweating. An antivenin is available for black widow stings and is often used in conjunction with narcotics to reduce the pain associated with the bite.

The brown recluse sometimes has a violin-shaped pattern on its abdomen, but a more reliable identifier is that the brown recluse has six eyes instead of the normal eight of most spiders. Unlike the black widow's venom, which is a neurotoxin, the brown recluse spider has hemotoxin venom that kills red blood cells and can lead to large tissue death around the wound site. The initial brown recluse bite is often not painful

Tarantulas are large spiders found in the southwestern United States.

and symptoms don't develop until twenty-four hours later. As a result, many other ailments are sometimes blamed on brown recluse bites, such as skin ulcers and staff infections. There is no effective treatment for recluse bites except to treat the resulting dead cell and tissue areas of the bite.

Backpackers in areas that are known to have high populations of black widow or brown recluse spiders can reduce their chances of being bitten by sleeping in tents and carefully checking their clothing and hiking boots for critters in the morning.

Scorpions

Scorpions are another member of the arachnid group to watch for in the backcountry. Scorpions, like the black widow and brown recluse spiders, are nocturnal and are commonly found throughout much of the Southwest. Scorpions have large pinchers and a stinger on the end of their trail. While deaths from scorpion bites are rare, the scorpion's sting is very painful, similar to a bee or hornet sting. Again, check your boots in the morning to shake out any scorpions.

Ticks

Ticks are parasites that feed on blood and are found in most temperate regions of the United States. They often live in tall grass or brush and attach themselves to passing mammals and birds. If they are not discovered and removed, ticks will fill themselves up with the host's blood and then drop off. While a tick bite in itself is more of a nuisance than a hazard, ticks are carriers of disease such as Lyme disease and Rocky Mountain spotted fever. Cases of Lyme disease have been documented in many areas of the United States, but the highest levels of infection are seen in the Eastern states. The disease often presents a host of symptoms, including red rash and high fever, and if left untreated can lead to joint pain and paralysis—even death. The American deer tick is one of the primary carriers of Lyme disease. The tick is very small, about the size of the head of a match. West of the Mississippi River, the most common species of tick people encounter is the American dog tick. The dog tick is larger, about the size of an eraser on a pencil. Dog ticks do not carry Lyme disease, but can carry Rocky Mountain spotted fever, which has symptoms similar to Lyme disease. If left untreated, it can also be fatal.

If you discover a tick on yourself or a friend, the most effective way to remove it is to use a pair of tweezers and slowly pull with increasing force until the tick lets go. To prevent being bitten by ticks, wear long-sleeve shirts and pants and tuck your pant legs into your socks or boots. Spraying exposed skin areas with a solution containing DEET will discourage ticks, but the best thing to do is to check yourself for ticks during rest breaks and more thoroughly at the end of the day.

HAZARD: INSECTS

Insects all have three body segments, three pairs of legs, and two antennae. There are many kinds of insects ranging from cockroaches to butterflies. Every backcountry traveler has at least one epic "bug" story, which is usually more about suffering mentally than physically, but a few species can be harmful to the outdoor traveler. Here we look at hazards associated with bees, hornets, wasps, biting flies, and fleas.

Bees, Hornets, and Wasps

If bees, hornets, wasps, and honeybees did not exist, neither would humans—because these insects pollinate the vast majority of the foods we eat. Most bees are not aggressive. People come into contact with bees, hornets, and wasps by either getting too close to their nests (or hives), or by leaving out food that attracts certain species of hornets. Bees such as honeybees and bumblebees have a stinger on the end of their abdomen; when they sting, the stinger and venom sack stay attached to their victim. As a result, the bee can only sting once and then dies a short time later. Hornets and wasps have a retractable stinger and can sting many times. Honeybees, hornets, and wasps build nests in hollow trees, on the underside of branches, and on rock overhangs. The observant traveler can avoid these hazards. However, some hornets like yellow jackets make their nests underground. The hiker is only aware of a

Hornets make nests out of paper-like material to protect their young.

nest after she inadvertently steps on one and a horde of angry hornets swarms around. The venom in a sting is very painful and causes swelling and redness. Some individuals develop an allergic reaction to bee stings. Symptoms include hives and difficult breathing, which are signs of a severe, whole-body allergic reaction, anaphylaxis, which is a life-threatening condition that needs to be treated immediately.

Steps to Avoid Confrontations with Stinging Insects

- » Avoid known nest and hive areas.
- » Seal smelly food items in plastic bags.
- » If stung, remove yourself from the area quickly. Bees, wasps, and hornets have a territory they will defend.
- » After vacating the area, pull the stinger out as soon as possible to reduce the venom injected.

Common Chemical Repellents for Arthropods

Repellent	Composition	Development	Side Effects	Effectiveness
Common Name: *DEET*	N,N-diethyl-m-toluamide or N,N-diethyl-3-methylbenzamide	U.S. Army during WWII; commercially available since 1950s in United States	Greasy feeling on skin, unpleasant smell, can melt plastic and synthetic clothing; despite years of study no side effects have been proven with short-term use	Very effective
Common Name: *Picaridin (KBR 3023)*	2-(2-hydrozyethyl-1-piper-idincarboxylic acid 1-methyl-propyl ester)	Developed in Europe, used in South America, Australia, Asia first; came to the United States in 2005	None known	Slightly less effective than DEET against some arthropods
Common Name: *Oil of lemon eucalyptus or PMD*	Para-methane-3,8-diol which is the synthesized version of oil of lemon eucalyptus	Natural, plant-based repellent oil that is prepared from leaves of Eucalyptus citriodora	Can be an eye irritant	Must be applied more frequently than DEET; as effective as DEET against mosquitoes

Common Name: Avon Skin So Soft, IR3535	3-[N-butyl-N-acetyl]-aminopropionic acid	Originally developed as beauty aid/skin softener	None known	10–100 percent less effective than similar concentration of DEET
Common Name: Citronella	Oils from the leaves and stems of different species of Cymbopogon, originally found in Sri Lanka and Java	First used in soaps and perfume	Some people develop skin irritation.	When used on the skin, slightly more effective than Skin So Soft, but needs to be reapplied every 20-60 minutes. Burned as a candle, it can keep some insects 1 meter away.

» People with known anaphylactic episodes should carry appropriate drugs such as epinephrine and antihistamines and know how to administer them.

The "Killer bee" or African honeybee is a non-native species that is very similar to our native honeybee. They are less tolerant to cold conditions, so their range is restricted to the Southwest. All bees will swarm a perceived threat to their nest or hives, but killer bees tend to be very aggressive in this behavior. Their sting is not any more potent than that of regular bees, but they will swarm and sting a perceived threat hundreds or thousands of times.

Blood-Sucking Flies

Mosquitoes are one of the most hated outdoor insect pests. From their annoying high whining wing buzz to their painful itchy bites, these creatures have caused generations of campers to lose sleep and return home with red welts all over their bodies. The female mosquito bites humans and other mammals to obtain blood to increase her egg production. In addition, mosquitoes and other biting insects like fleas can act as hosts for a number of diseases such as malaria and bubonic plague, diseases that have been eradicated in the United States but are still common killers worldwide. Recently however, a new virus carried by mosquitoes, West Nile virus, has spread across the country causing flu-like symptoms in adults and some deaths among children and elderly people. Other biting insects range from large horse flies, deer flies, and black flies to tiny "no-see-um" midges.

The best way to deal with biting and bothersome arthropods is to cover up with clothing, hats, gloves, and even a head net when the number of critters is really large. But what if the temperature is 80 degrees with 100 percent humidity? There are a number of commercially available repellents. Several factors come into play in terms of how effective repellents are against arthropods, including how often you apply the repellent, how much you are sweating, whether it is rainy or windy, and how attractive your "smell" is to arthropods like mosquitoes.

HAZARD: MICROSCOPIC ORGANISMS

Although you cannot see microscopic hazards such as bacteria, virus, and protozoans, you can certainly feel the effects in your body once they take hold. The most common way these small creatures get inside us is through eating and drinking. Two parasitic hazards hikers are often concerned about are Giardia amebae and Cryptosporidium. The cyst (eggs) of these protozoans get into water sources from fecal contamination by mammals infected with the disease. Any mammal can carry the cysts, including,

Make sure to treat water from suspect sources in the backcountry.

cattle, moose, beavers, as well as people. These one-celled organisms are found throughout the world and in many water sources; even public drinking water may contain very low levels of the cysts. The cysts of Giardia and Cryptosporidium hatch inside the small intestines and cause diarrhea, fever, nausea, vomiting, and abdominal pain. Some people will recover in a few weeks, but most will need medication to combat the parasite.

One-Celled Hazard	Purification Technique			
	Heat	Filtration	Chemical	UV Light
Virus: *Hep A*	Yes	Maybe; need filter that also has some type of chemical treatment	Iodine Chlorine: Yes	Yes; need clear water
Bacteria: *E. Coli, Salmonella*	Yes	Maybe; need 0.3 micron filter or smaller	Iodine Chlorine: Yes	Yes; need clear water
Protozoa: *Giardia amebae*	Yes	Yes; need 1 micron filter or smaller	Iodine Chlorine: Yes	Yes; need clear water
Protozoa: *Cryptosporidium*	Yes	Maybe; need 0.3 micron filter or smaller	Iodine Chlorine: No	Yes; need clear water

Prevention is easy. Wash or sanitize your hands before eating or cooking, treat suspect drinking water, and cook all food thoroughly. You can treat questionable water sources several ways. Boiling, filtering, and chemical treatments are all viable options.

Chemical treatments to purify water are fast and effective against most pathogens.

Chapter Eleven
Plants

Hiking along the Appalachian Trail in the early fall while the leaves are turning provides you with an inspiring kaleidoscope of colors. However, bushwhacking through a dense stand of willow and slide alders in Boston Basin in Washington's North Cascades often leaves you sweating and cursing. All plants are not created equal in terms of backcountry enjoyment and some can be hazardous to your health.

HAZARD: BUSHWHACKING

Off-trail travel adds problem solving and the excitement of the unknown into your backcountry experiences. However, when you are bushwhacking, you can do a number of things to make the experience

Almost all plants in the desert have some type of thorn like this ocotillo.

safer and more enjoyable. First, get ready for your off-trail adventure by making your pack stream-lined. Take items that are clipped or strapped to the outside of the backpack, such as water bottles and sleeping pads, and pack them inside. Put on a long sleeve shirt and pants to protect yourself from abra-sions. Consider wearing sunglasses to protect your eyes and gloves to protect your hands. Know what types of plants you are going to encounter, so you do not inadvertently grab a branch to keep your balance and end up with a handful of thorns. While navigating through thick vegetation, try to keep enough distance between you and your hiking partners so you do not get hit by "fly back" branches.

HAZARD: POISONOUS PLANTS

While ingesting poisonous plants can be a serious backcountry hazard, it is totally preventable by sim-ply not eating any plant that you do not know the exact identity of. However, some other poisonous plants can still cause problems for the wilderness traveler. If you spend enough time walking around in the woods, you will most likely develop a rash on your skin as the result of contact with one of these three plants: poison sumac, poison ivy, and poison oak. All three of these plants contain urushiol oil, which is a potent skin irritator in small quantities. Poison sumac is an uncommon shrub that is found in very

Poison ivy has leaves in groups of three.

Even dead poison ivy still contains the oils that irritate skin.

wet areas in the Southeast. Poison oak and poison ivy can grow as ground cover, vines, or shrubs and are found throughout North America. They have leaves in groups of three and can sometimes display a shiny luster on the leaves. After just a few minutes of direct skin contact with one of these plants, the oils are bonded to your skin and a very itchy rash develops. The best treatment is to wash the affected area with soap and water to remove the oil and not scratch the rash, which can cause scarring. Once the oil has been removed, the rash cannot spread to other areas of your body or to another person, and after a week or two it will disappear on its own. To reduce the itching, dermatologists recommend oatmeal baths or putting baking soda on the rash.

HAZARD: DEAD SNAGS AND WIDOW MAKERS

When selecting a campsite for the evening, there are many things you should take into consideration to increase your comfort and reduce your environmental impact. These include camping at least a few hundred feet from a trail and water source and looking for a flat site that has been used before, or if not previously used, that is on a durable surface. One thing most people do not do is look up into the tree canopy to see if there are any dead branches or limbs that might fall on their tent during the night. In

Watch out for dead trees or branches overhead when setting up your tent.

established campsites, other users may have killed or weakened the trees by girdling the bark or by cutting off branches for firewood. Even in remote areas, dead trees caused by insect infestations can quickly change a nice sheltered spot into a potentially deadly campsite during high winds. Early fall snow storms, while the leaves are still on the trees, can take down even living branches and trees. The leaves allow more snow and weight to accumulate. An early snow event might be hard for you to plan for in advance, but once it is happening, you should move your camp to a safe location.

Chapter Twelve

Humans

HAZARD: OTHER PEOPLE IN THE OUTDOORS

Other visitors recreating in the same wild region can be potential hazards. These visitors might be doing the same type of activity as you, such climbing on the same rock face, or they might be participating in a different activity like snowmobiling or cross-country skiing but sharing the same terrain. Before you go into the backcountry, part of your research should be to find out what other types of users recreate in the region. Often, if the speed of the activity in the shared terrain is very different, problems and dangers arise. Some public lands will allow only certain activities and might even suggest trail etiquette for different types of user groups. In many locations horses, hikers, and mountain bikers will share the same trail. The common and sometimes posted rule states that bikers should yield to hikers, and hikers and bikers should both yield to horses. This rule is based on the speed and maneuverability of the activities. If you do encounter horses while hiking on a trail, step off on the downside and let the horses pass. Horses will feel more comfortable, as they tend to go uphill when spooked or frightened.

Dogs

Dogs are one hazard associated with other people. Some areas require dogs to be on a leash at all times, some do not, but all canine owners are

Some dogs are friendly, while others can be aggressive in the backcountry. Use caution.

expected to be able to control their dog. Dogs are naturally territorial and protective of their owners and some get confused about how much territory they need to protect. They will aggressively defend a section of the trail by barking as you approach. Usually talking to the dog in a calm manner will diffuse the situation. However, if you feel the dog is going to attack, defend yourself with trekking poles, sticks, rocks, even pepper spray. Often, quickly taking off your pack and holding it in front of you will provide protection from a dog attack until the owner can get control of his animal.

Hunters

Hunting is a popular activity on many public lands. Almost every state requires new hunters to take a hunting safety course that helps prevent conflicts and accidents with other users. However, there are several things you can do to increase your safety when interacting with hunters. First, know what type of hunting season is in effect for the area you are visiting and when and where they occur. That way you can predict in what type of terrain you might encounter a hunter and what time of day they will be most active. Second, make yourself known by wearing blaze orange vests, hats, and other clothing. Make noise to alert hunters of your presence and do not wear camouflage.

Either wear or strap to your pack some blaze orange during hunting season to make yourself more visible.

Criminal Element

There have been a few accounts of theft and even violence directed toward hikers in the backcountry. However, these incidents are extremely rare. Crime, when it does happen, usually occurs near the trailhead. Criminals aren't likely to hike a long way into the wilderness because there are few potential victims in there. Also, criminals typically seek out victims they can easily overpower and then quickly leave the area, which is not an option deep in the wilderness.

There are self-defense options for the solo traveler, such as hiking with a dog, carrying pepper spray, or even a gun. Make sure you have proper knowledge of how to safely use a firearm and what permits are necessary to carry a gun in the area you are visiting. The easiest and potentially most enjoyable way to make yourself safer when hiking is to invite a few friends along. The more people in your group, the less likely you are to be the target of crime.

Break-ins at trailheads are the most common type of criminal activity that affects hikers. Don't leave valuables in your car!

Chapter Thirteen

Outdoor Technology and Being Safe

Despite all of your planning and preparation before you head out into the wilderness, things can still go wrong. As this book has made clear, there are a number of hazards that can affect your experience: Weather conditions can change, you can get lost or injured, or a bear could eat all of your food. Luckily help is just a call away—or is it? GPS units, cell phones, satellite phones, and personal locating devices have all increased connection to the outside world. There is no doubt the availability of new communication technology has saved lives and in some cases even prevented unnecessary rescues. Unfortunately, calling for a rescue in situations where one is unnecessary has become much more common as the result of this technology. Real threats to life and limb are instances in which calling for search and rescue is completely justified. Being late for work or not feeling like walking any farther are not.

Being flexible and resourceful and using all the tools available are skills of a seasoned outdoor traveler. But the most important tool is still your brain. Before you head into the backcountry, tell someone else where you are going and when you plan to be back. Bring your cell phone along to call and update the plan if need be. Use your GPS, but make sure you have a set of maps and know how to interpret

Technology can be helpful in the backcountry, but it can also get in the way of your wilderness experience.

them and use a compass. Use your smart phone to get updates on the weather forecast, but balance that against your observations of the clouds you see in the atmosphere. Purchase the latest sticky rubber for your approach shoes, but make sure you have the basic rock climbing movement techniques down before you go scrambling in the mountains.

One way to analyze outdoor hazards is to look at the probability of something bad happening and the consequences of that event. For example, what would you do if you and your friends were halfway through a weeklong backpacking loop and came to an exposed section of trail that was only two feet wide with a 1,000-foot drop off with no railing or other barrier? The likelihood of an experienced hiker falling off a two-foot-wide trail is low—but if you did fall, you would certainly die. Would you continue and complete the trip, or return the way you came? The next scenario is the same, but instead of a sheer cliff there is a long section of trail that is covered with poison ivy, making the likelihood of getting a poison ivy rash very high. But are the consequences high enough to make you backtrack?

There is no right answer to the questions posed in these scenarios. Assessing the probability of an accident and the consequences of the accident are part of the analysis of risk every hiker must perform in the backcountry.

For some people the anxiety of reading a book on outdoor hazards might make them take up knitting and forget venturing into the backcountry. Hopefully, by defining the hazards and giving suggestions for how to reduce the dangers, this book will help most wilderness travelers feel more confident in making decisions about the outdoor hazards they might face during their next adventure.

Everything that is worthwhile in life entails some risk—that's what makes life so interesting. It sounds like a cliché, but statistics show that you are much more likely to be injured in a car accident on the way to the trailhead than on the hike itself. Some people might ask, Why not stay inside and avoid exposing yourself to unnecessary outdoor hazards in the first place? Well, consider the fact that the leading cause of death in the United States is heart disease—usually the result of not taking care of our bodies and getting enough exercise. So sitting inside does not seem to be the answer to living a long life. Enjoy yourself, get outside, and be safe!

INDEX

ABOUT THE AUTHOR

Dave Anderson has worked as a guide for the past twenty-five years leading many different types of outdoor pursuits, including natural history treks, wilderness backpacking, rock climbing, ice climbing, mountaineering, white water rafting, and canoeing. Dave is also a senior instructor for the National Outdoor Leadership School (NOLS), where he teaches rock climbing and mountaineering courses, develops curriculum, and conducts staff trainings.

In addition, Dave has been a professional photographer and writer for the past fifteen years. His work has appeared in various publications such as *National Geographic,* the *New York Times, Sports Illustrated, INC Magazine, Alpinist, Patagonia, Black Diamond,* the *American Alpine Journal,* as well as several books by Globe Pequot Press/FalconGuides. He is the author of the upcoming book *Expedition Planning.*

Dave is also a motivational speaker and has given over 200 multimedia presentations about his climbing accomplishments and interactions with remote cultures. He has been the keynote speaker at the Western Regional Outdoor Leadership Conference and Wilderness Medical Society, and he has given lectures at prestigious universities such as Yale, Harvard, and the Naval Academy.